30 Fun Ways to Learn with Blocks and Boxes

by Clare Beswick

With contributions from
Lisa Chichester of Parkersburg, West Virginia;
Marilyn Harding of Grimes, Kentucky;
Ann Kelly of Johnstown, Pennsylvania;
Amy Melisi of Oxford, Massachusetts; and
Bev Schumacher of Ft. Mitchell, Kentucky.

30 FUN WAYS to Learn with BLOCKS AND BOXES

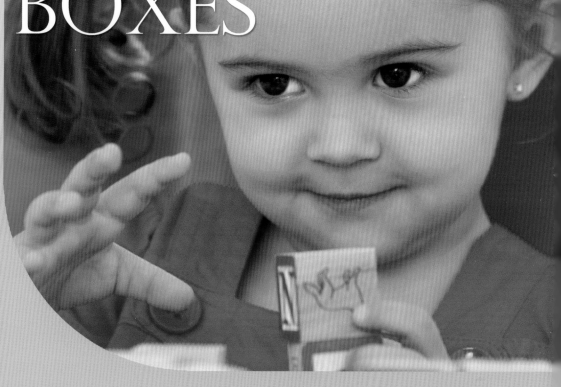

CLARE BESWICK
ILLUSTRATED BY K. WHELAN DERY

© 2011 Gryphon House, Inc.
Published by Gryphon House, Inc.
10770 Columbia Pike, Suite 201
Silver Spring, MD 20901
800.638.0928; 301.595.9500; 301.595.0051 (fax)

Visit us on the web at www.gryphonhouse.com

Originally published in 2003 by Featherstone Education.

Illustrations: K. Whelan Dery
Cover Art: © iStockphoto LP 2009. All rights reserved. iStockphoto® and iStock® are trademarks of iStockphoto LP. Flash® is a registered trademark of Adobe Inc. www.istockphoto.com.

Many thanks to Belleville Primary School

Library of Congress Cataloging-in-Publication Data
30 fun ways to learn with blocks and boxes / by Clare Beswick, [editor].
    p. cm.
  ISBN 978-0-87659-369-1
  1. Blocks (Toys)—Juvenile literature. 2. Boxes—Juvenile literature. I. Beswick, Clare. II. Title: Thirty fun ways to learn about blocks and boxes.
  GV1218.B6A27 2011
  790.1'33--dc22
                            2010045547

Bulk purchase
Gryphon House books are available for special premiums and sales promotions as well as for fund-raising use. Special editions or book excerpts also can be created to specification. For details, contact the Director of Marketing at Gryphon House.

Disclaimer
Gryphon House, Inc. and the author cannot be held responsible for damage, mishap, or injury incurred during the use of or because of activities in this book. Appropriate and reasonable caution and adult supervision of children involved in activities and corresponding to the age and capability of each child involved is recommended at all times. Do not leave children unattended at any time. Observe safety and caution at all times.

Contents

Introduction

This book provides fun, easy-to-do construction activities, using everyday materials. It is intended for everyone working with young children in schools, child care settings, preschools, or at home.

The activities are:

- Planned to help children move toward early learning goals.
- Practical and fun.
- Designed to build on children's natural curiosity.
- Easily adaptable for children at different developmental stages.
- Ideal for small groups or for individual children.

Each activity meets a range of goals. These are listed on each page, along with the materials you will need, clear instructions, and helpful tips and hints. You will find additional ideas on each page to extend or adapt the original activity, or to help you develop new activities using similar materials.

Why Blocks and Boxes?

Construction play is an important part of early childhood. Children are fascinated by blocks and the endless possibilities offered by construction materials. From the first tower knocked over to collaborative construction using a range of materials over an extended period, children are drawn to building activities that enliven their imaginations.

Using blocks and boxes, children can test their ideas about the way the world works and how and why things happen. They can express their creativity, develop their imaginations, and play! Blocks and boxes can be used to extend play in all areas: from sand and water and working with clay, to outdoor play, language, mathematical exploration, and so much more. Children learn about space and shapes and how things fit together. They practice using tools and manipulating objects. Try out some of the activities in this book to make the most of blocks and boxes in your setting.

Learning Objectives

Constructing and playing with blocks and boxes contributes to the following learning objectives.

Personal, Social, and Emotional Development

Children:

- Work as part of a group or class, taking turns and sharing.
- Interact with others, negotiating plans and activities.
- Maintain attention and concentration when necessary.
- Are interested, excited, and motivated to learn.

Communication, Language, and Literacy

Children:

- Use a widening vocabulary to express their ideas and observations.
- Express and communicate ideas about designing and making.
- Link sounds and letters.
- Use language that expresses direction: up/down; over/under; in/out.

Problem Solving, Reasoning, and Numeracy

Children:

- Use mathematical language in play. (For example: lighter/heavier; more/less; bigger/smaller.)
- Say and understand number names.
- Talk about, recognize, and recreate simple patterns.
- Use language such as "circle" or "bigger" to describe the shape and comparative sizes of solids and
  flat shapes.
- Recognize numerals from 1 to 9.

Knowledge and Understanding of the World

Children:

- Use simple tools and techniques competently and appropriately.
- Build and construct with a wide range of objects, selecting appropriate materials and adapting work where necessary.
- Investigate objects and materials by using all of their senses.
- Look closely at similarities and differences.
- Observe the places where they live.

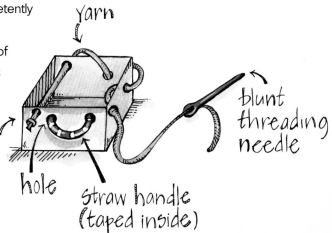

Physical Development

Children:

- Use a range of materials with increasing control.
- Develop their hand-eye coordination.
- Dress and undress with increasing independence.
- Move in a range of ways.

Creative Development

Children:

- Explore color, texture, and form.
- Design and make things.

Activities with Blocks and Boxes

brick wall

Lego wall

stone wall

pebbles

large appliance box

envelope

checking address

sticky notes

521

mail slot

1 Tower Blocks

Build tall towers, practice taking turns, and play cooperatively in pairs.

Vocabulary

blocks
build
buildings
fall
high/higher
measure
take turns
tall/taller
tower

What you need

- building blocks
- pens
- ribbon
- scissors (adult use only)
- sticky notes
- 2 boxes (for the blocks)

Learning objectives

Children will:

- Maintain attention and concentration when necessary.
- Interact with others, negotiating plans and activities.
- Use mathematical language in play.
- Talk about, recognize, and recreate simple patterns.
- Develop their hand-eye coordination.

Before you start

Take a look at pictures of really tall towers. What are they used for? Talk about power stations, towers at fire stations, tall office buildings, and apartment buildings.

Helpful hint

Play this game on the floor, with lots of different types of blocks, stacking toys, or boxes. Adjust your materials to the ages of your children.

post-it   ribbon

Nate

What you do

1. Divide the blocks between the two boxes. Help two children write their names on sticky notes.
2. Let the younger child place the first block. Take turns adding blocks to the tower. Try to keep it from falling down! Use simple repetitive instructions to help with the turn-taking, such as "Joe's turn," "Amy's turn," and so on.
3. Attach the name labels to the last block of the tower. Cut a length of ribbon the same height as the tower.
4. Knock down the tower together and then see if you can use different blocks to build another tower the same height.

More ideas

- Use the sticky notes to number each floor of the tower.
- Sort the blocks to make towers of different colors, or repeating patterns of colors.
- Cut a length of ribbon and guess how many blocks will be needed to build a tower of that height.
- Use blocks and paint to print towers and walls on large paper.
- Try building towers with blocks in the sand or water trays.
- Build towers with coins or buttons to practice fine motor skills, as well as turn-taking. Safety note: Supervise closely when you are using these very small objects.

Giant Junk Models

2

Construct on a huge scale to create imaginative play spaces.

Vocabulary

build

duct tape

fasten

flexible

guttering

heavy

huge

join

pipe

What you need

- duct tape, string, clips
- hula hoops
- large cardboard boxes
- lengths of flexible pipe
- old blankets or sheets
- plastic rain guttering
- sheets of bubble wrap
- tires

Learning objectives

Children will:

- Work as part of a group or class, taking turns and sharing.
- Interact with others, negotiating plans and activities.
- Use mathematical language in their play.
- Build and construct with a wide range of objects, selecting appropriate materials and adapting work where necessary.

Before you start

Visit your local garden center and home improvement store for ideas. Ask families to suggest or bring in suitable building materials.

What you do

1 Talk with the children about the building materials. Think about how they might be fastened together. Give the children plenty of time to explore the materials.

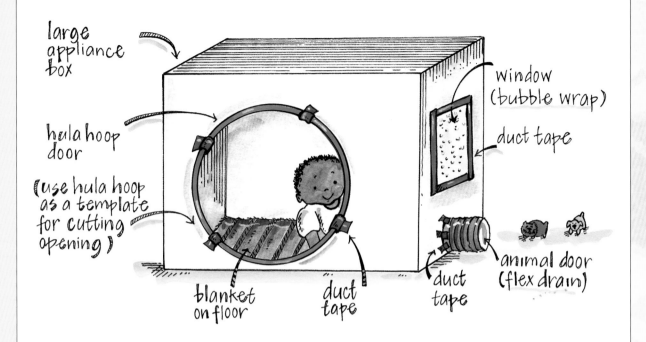

large appliance box

hula hoop door

(use hula hoop as a template for cutting opening)

window (bubble wrap)

duct tape

blanket on floor

duct tape

duct tape

animal door (flex drain)

② Listen carefully as the children talk. Ask open-ended questions as they develop their ideas of what to build. Help them develop their plans, as needed.

③ Encourage the children to work together to build one structure or den. Add or offer additional resources and props as needed or requested by the children.

④ Help with joining and balancing the building materials, but always ask the children for their ideas about how their plans can be achieved or adapted.

More ideas

- Add a silver foil survival blanket (from a camping store) to create a rocket or a space station.
- Provide child-sized wheelbarrows, wagons, and carts to move the building materials around.
- Add some builder's hats, reflective vests, and other dress-up clothes for the building site.
- Make some warning triangles, notices, and other signs for the building site.
- Visit a home improvement store to look at building materials, wood, plastic, metal, brick, and other materials.
- Get some life-sized wooden or plastic bricks to build walls.

Will It Sink?

Large and small, heavy and light—explore floating and sinking with blocks and boxes.

Vocabulary

balance

balsa wood

count

experiment

float

heavy

light

load

raft

sink

What you need

- balsa wood scraps
- buttons
- coins
- individual water trays (large bowls or dishpans work well)
- plastic packaging trays, well-washed
- Styrofoam scraps (not too small)
- variety of plastic blocks of different sizes
- waterproof tape (duct tape is good)

Learning objectives

Children will:

- Be interested, excited, and motivated to learn.
- Use a widening vocabulary to express their ideas.
- Say and understand number names.
- Investigate objects and materials by using all of their senses.
- Use a range of small and large materials.
- Express and communicate ideas about designing and making.

Before you start

Ask families to save and send in clean packaging materials.

Safety note: Supervise carefully. Make sure children do not put things in their mouths.

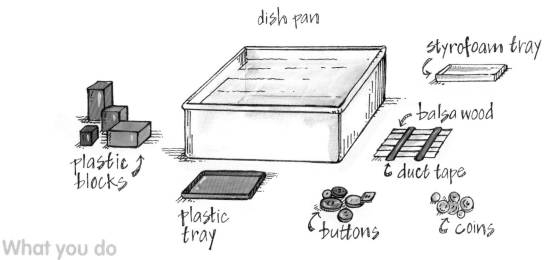

dish pan

styrofoam tray

balsa wood

duct tape

plastic blocks

plastic tray

buttons

coins

What you do

1. Let the children explore the materials and discover how they behave in water.

2. Talk with the children about constructing rafts from the balsa wood, Styrofoam, and plastic packaging.

3. Encourage each child to construct a small raft, using an assortment of materials.

4. See how many blocks, coins, buttons, or other small objects can be loaded onto the rafts before they sink. Help the children count them, if they need help. Does it make a difference where you put the objects on the raft?

5. Watch the objects as they fall off the raft. Which ones float and which ones sink? Could you build another raft, using the ones that float?

6. Give the children plenty of unhurried time to explore this activity in depth and test out their own ideas and theories.

More ideas

- Add play people to the rafts.
- Put some small, heavy objects (such as pebbles and paper clips) in plastic containers. Do these float? Put lots of light things (such as feathers, cotton balls, and packing peanuts) in bigger containers. Can you load these on the rafts? Do they float? Try any other explorations that occur to you and the children.
- Can you build a tower that is heavy enough to stand up on the bottom of the water tray? Does loading it with heavy objects help?
- Experiment with adding other things to the water, such as food coloring, ice, cornstarch. What changes do the children notice?

4 Construction Site

Block play takes on another dimension in a child-sized construction site.

Vocabulary

bridge

build

buildings

construction

damp

highway

mold

pile

road

sand

What you need

- little yogurt containers
- paper towel tubes
- pebbles
- play people
- popsicle sticks
- sand tray/builder's tray
- shoeboxes
- small plastic blocks such as Legos®
- toy diggers and dump trucks

Learning objectives

Children will:

- Be confident to try new activities.
- Talk about, recognize, and recreate simple patterns.
- Use a range of materials with increasing control.
- Use simple tools and techniques competently and appropriately.
- Explore color, texture, and form.

Before you start

Make the sand thoroughly damp by adding warm water and mixing well. Sing building songs such as "This Is the Way We Build a House" to the tune of "Here We Go 'Round the Mulberry Bush."

Helpful hint

Always use clean play sand (builder's sand, although cheaper, contains dyes that may irritate the skin and stain clothes or furniture).

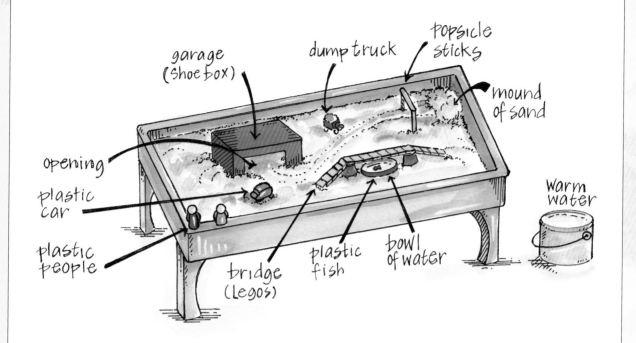

garage
(shoe box)

dump truck

popsicle
sticks

mound
of sand

opening

plastic
car

plastic
people

bridge
(Legos)

plastic
fish

bowl
of water

warm
water

What you do

1. Set up the sand tray with blocks, toy vehicles, and play people. Start the children off by showing them how to make a simple building. Then encourage them to make their own.
2. Add the shoeboxes, popsicle sticks, and cardboard tubes as building materials.
3. Use the small yogurt containers as molds, filling and turning out the sand.
4. Encourage the children to combine the different materials to make buildings (for example, use plastic blocks with the popsicle sticks and tubes).

More ideas

- Add toy cars and build a road, highway, or bridge. Use string, scissors, and glue to create more elaborate model buildings in the sand.
- Help the children cut the cardboard tubes and boxes to create the shapes they need.
- Add objects for printing patterns in the sand—for example, a roller to create a roadway, tires for tracks, spools, blocks, and so on.
- Make a large building site outside.
- Visit a real building site if you can, to enhance the children's play.

Walls and ...?

We quickly think of towers and roads when we think of children working with blocks. But what about other kinds of structures made of block-like building materials? Offer pictures and see what happens.

Vocabulary

ancient
block
brick
build/builders
China
engineering
fence
long ago
wall
worker

What you need

- blocks
- pictures of walls in different contexts

Learning objectives

Children will:

- Work as part of a group or class, taking turns and sharing.
- Interact with others, negotiating plans and activities.
- Use a widening vocabulary to express their ideas and observations.
- Express and communicate ideas about designing and making.
- Build and construct, selecting appropriate materials and adapting work where necessary.

Before you start

Collect pictures and books about famous walls around the world and throughout history. Plan a local walk to look at walls in different contexts.

What you do

1. Take a walk around the neighborhood and notice the kinds of walls you see. Do you have a wall around your schoolyard?
2. Talk about walls and fences and the different purposes they serve.
3. Hang pictures of walls in the block area. Some suggestions would be: the Great Wall of China, old stone walls in New England, or a wall near your home—anything that appeals to you and that you think would be interesting to the children.

④ Let the children take it from there. Add toy animals and people if the play seems to be moving in that direction.

⑤ Use the books that you found to answer questions and to enlarge the context for the building projects.

More ideas

● After talking about and building the Great Wall of China, serve fortune cookies for a snack.

● Sing or recite "Humpty Dumpty sat on a wall . . ." at circle time, or any time, just for fun.

● Broaden the exploration: introduce pictures and books about the Pyramids of Egypt and encourage the children to try building pyramids. Pyramids take a lot of blocks!

● Look on the Internet or at the library for reproductions of the work of the artists Andrew Goldsworthy, or of Christo and Jeanne-Claude. Their work can be inspiring to wall-builders.

Blueprint Books

6

Introduce the children to the idea of a visual record of the construction process.

Vocabulary

architect
blueprint
construction
contractor
directions
floor
guide
layer
page numbers
worker

What you need

- blocks
- construction paper the same color as the blocks
- drawing paper, sheets of various sizes
- glue
- markers
- scissors (adult use only)
- stapler

colored construction paper

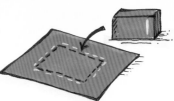

Learning objectives

Children will:

- Use a widening vocabulary to express their ideas and observations.
- Express and communicate ideas about designing and making.
- Talk about, recognize, and recreate simple patterns.
- Look closely at similarities and differences.
- Say and understand number names.

Before you start

Trace the different shapes of your blocks onto matching construction paper. Cut them out. Make sure you have plenty of each shape available.

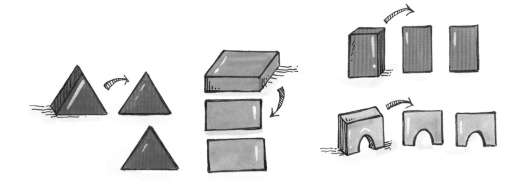

What you do

1. Sit with a child in the block center and ask if you may make a "blueprint" of her block creation. Proceed if given permission.

2. Recreate the child's work by gluing cutouts of the blocks that match the first layer of the child's building on a piece of paper.

3. Repeat this process on a new piece of paper for the second layer of blocks. Continue with a new sheet of paper for each layer of the child's building. Number the pages as you go.

4. Let the child name her creation and make a cover for the blueprint book. Staple all the pages together.

5. If there are enough blocks, recreate the building using the blueprint book as a guide. Encourage the child or children to compare the buildings as they build the second one.

More ideas

- Leave the materials in the block area for the children to make their own blueprint books. (Some children will need more assistance than others.)
- Leave the blueprint books in the block area for other children to follow.
- Read *How Our House Works* by Larry Burkett with the children.

Natural Builder

Encourage imaginations to soar with building materials from the natural world.

Vocabulary

bark

build

ferns

leaves

raffia

scene

straw

texture

twigs

twine

What you need

- bark, ferns, and leaves
- clay
- corks and sponges
- pebbles and stones
- raffia and dried grass
- seed heads and grasses
- shells
- shoeboxes and lids (1 per child)
- twigs and small sticks
- wood and wood shavings

Learning objectives

Children will:

- Be interested, excited, and motivated to learn.
- Interact with others, negotiating plans and activities.
- Investigate objects and materials using all their senses.
- Use a range of tools and materials with increasing control.
- Explore color, texture, and shape.

Before you start

Ask families and children to collect and bring in materials and shoeboxes. Visit the park and collect materials. Try your local florist or garden center for ideas. They may be able to give you prunings, clippings, or other interesting scraps.

Helpful hint

Leaves are great for building. Use different textures and sizes. Use a big shallow tray for the group, or shoebox lids for individual children.

corks
bark
ferns
leaves
sponge
shoebox
lid
pebbles and stones
grass
twigs

What you do

1 Collect your materials and put them in containers for easy access.

2 Talk about the materials. Look at the colors, shapes, and textures and talk about where different things came from.

3 Give each of the children a shoebox and encourage them to create scenes inside their boxes. Allow plenty of time to explore and build. Add toy people, animals, or small vehicles to extend the play.

4 Help the children experiment with balancing the materials or joining them up. Provide twine, raffia, or grass stems for tying.

5 The children may want to use dough, clay, or sand as a base for their constructions.

6 Leave the materials out for the children to return to again and again.

More ideas

- Do a giant class version outside with sticks and twigs, grasses, and fern fronds. Add pieces of garden netting.
- Try painting with the natural materials.
- Use the materials in wet sand and add containers to use for molds.
- Make caves, tree houses, and dens for play people and animals.
- Read animal stories and make homes for the characters.
- Read the story of "The Three Little Pigs" and encourage the children to make the pigs' houses from straw and twigs.
- Make homes, shelters, and nests for animals to live or hibernate in.

Rocket Launch

Make some rockets from recycled and throw-away materials, and fly into space!

Vocabulary

astronaut
booster
cone
cylinder
engine
explore
fuel
orbit
planet
rocket
space

What you need

Materials of your choice, including

- aluminium foil
- bottle tops
- card stock
- cardboard boxes and tubes
- child-safe scissors
- clear plastic bottles
- clothespins
- cylindrical containers from snack food
- glue
- paper clips
- plastic containers
- string
- tape

Learning objectives

Children will:

- Build and construct with a wide range of objects, selecting appropriate materials and adapting work where necessary.
- Interact with others, negotiating plans and activities.
- Use words, such as "circle" or "bigger," to describe the shapes and comparative sizes of solids and flat shapes.
- Use simple tools and techniques competently and appropriately.
- Explore color, texture, and form.

Before you start

Visit the library for stories about space and rockets, such as *On the Moon* by Ana Milbourne and *I Want to Be an Astronaut* by Byron Barton, and nonfiction books about space and rockets, such as *First Space Encyclopedia* by Caroline Bingham, or *Exploring Space* by Toni Eugene.

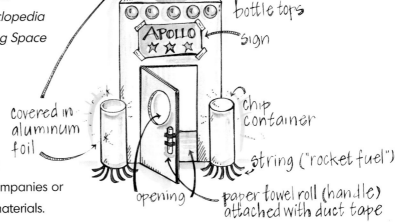

- cone (construction paper)
- ice cream container with lid
- bottle tops
- sign
- chip container
- string ("rocket fuel")
- paper towel roll (handle) attached with duct tape
- opening
- covered in aluminum foil

APOLLO ☆ ☆ ☆

Helpful hint

Check out your local hardware store, pet store, or home improvement store for additional materials. Try local packaging companies or recycling centers for recyclable materials.

What you do

1. Look at the books and tell the stories.
2. Talk about all the materials you have collected. Look for shapes and possible uses.
3. Talk about the different parts of the rockets—for example, boosters, cones, and engines.
4. Encourage each child to design and make her own rocket. Help her if she needs it, but do not interfere. Suggest different ways of attaching the pieces together.
5. Display the rockets, hanging them from the ceiling or a clothesline with string and clothespins.
6. Make some stars, moons, and planets and hang them as well.

More ideas

- Sponge silver paint on black paper. Use this to make cylinders for more rockets.
- Make rocket, robot, and spaceship shapes out of blocks.
- Offer some stickers and markers to make windows, doors, and other details.
- Use black paint on the inside of a large box to make a dark scene. Suspend rocket ships inside, decorate them with shiny stars and moons, and shine flashlights on the scene.
- Suggest that the children make a control panel from a flat box with buttons, dials, numbers, and a viewing monitor (from foil).

9 Heavy and Light

Begin to explore the concepts of weight and mass with these materials.

Vocabulary

balance
heavy/heavier
light/lighter
order
scale
weigh
weight

What you need

- bag of apples
- boxes of cereal, rice, and pasta
- colander
- cutlery
- plastic jug
- pots and pans
- simple scales
- 2 or more shoeboxes

Learning objectives

Children will:

- Work as part of a group or class, taking turns and sharing.
- Use mathematical language in play. (For example: lighter/heavier; more/less; bigger/smaller.)

Before you start

Give the children plenty of time to experiment with the scales. Talk about and look for different kinds of scales—for example, bathroom scales, kitchen scales, supermarket scales, and a balance scale.

Helpful hint

Try linking this free weighing activity with themes, for example: health, grocery store, or measurement.

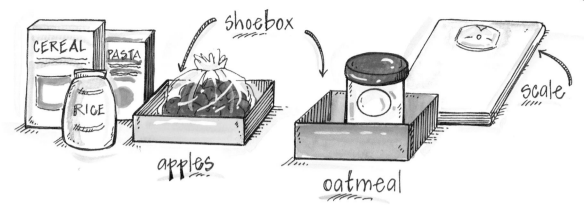

What you do

1. Put an object in each box. Ask the children to feel the weight of the boxes. Which is heavier? Which is lighter? (Hold one in each hand, as though your body were a simple balance scale.) Open the boxes and feel the weight of the objects themselves. Do plenty of this activity before moving on.

2. Next, choose a heavy item for one box, such as a bag of rice. Challenge the children to put items in the other box until it is the same weight as the rice. Older children could check with the scale.

3. Try putting objects in three boxes and guessing first which is heaviest.

4. Put objects in several different boxes. Can you work together to order the boxes by weight? Check the scale.

More ideas

- Take a trip to the post office and weigh a package, or take a trip to the supermarket and weigh some fruit for snack in the produce section.

- Ask a pediatric nurse to visit with a baby scale. If possible, invite a parent to bring in a baby brother or sister to be weighed. Talk about why we weigh babies. Weigh some dolls and teddy bears.

- Offer scales in the dramatic play area for weighing fruit, vegetables, and other shopping. They can also be used for a pretend baby clinic, post office, or vet.

- Have a set of scales and a basket of interesting objects for exploration (include small, heavy objects and big, light ones). Provide some paper and a clipboard for recording and mark making. Children also love putting things in paper bags!

- Wash the apples and then serve them for snack or lunch. Consider donating the boxes of cereal, rice, and pasta to a food pantry, or use the contents to make snack or lunch food for the children.

10 In the Wheelbarrow

Move the blocks with a wheelbarrow to build a wall. The children practice counting as they develop large motor skills and hand-eye coordination.

Vocabulary

block
brick
build
cement
count
mortar
path
straight
wall
wobble

What you need

- chalk
- child-sized wheelbarrows or wagons
- floor die
- large building blocks—plastic, wood, or cardboard
- paper, pens, clipboards, or whiteboards
- tape, if you do not use chalk (use masking tape for inside, duct tape for outside)

Learning objectives

Children will:

- Say and understand number names.
- Recognize numerals from 1 to 9.
- Develop their hand-eye coordination.
- Use mathematical language in play.

Before you start

Take a walk and look for brick walls. Count the rows and look at the brick patterns. Talk about how they stick together. Pay a visit to a home and garden center and look at some loose bricks.

Helpful hint

Shoeboxes with lids make good improvised bricks. Use brown paint and sponge print them, adding some sand to the paint.

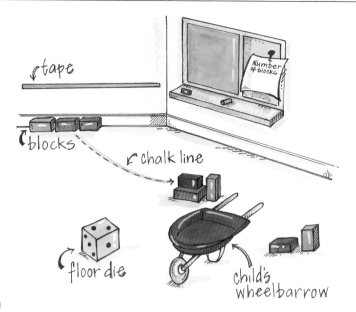

tape
Number of blocks
blocks
chalk line
floor die
child's wheelbarrow

What you do

1. Mark off the length of the wall you will build with chalk or tape. Chalk a path from the wall to the pile of bricks.
2. Let the children take turns rolling the big die, counting the dots, and putting that number of blocks in the wheelbarrow.
3. Then push the wheelbarrow along the path and add the blocks to the wall, trying not to wobble off the path. Offer help if it is needed.
4. As the wall grows, count each row as it is added; every so often, count the total number of blocks you have used. Help the children record this, supporting their own ways of making the record.
5. Tape the record to the top of the wall when it is finished.

More ideas

- Fill the wheelbarrow with blocks and wheel it along the path to the end. Roll the die and tip out the right number of blocks before returning along the path. Continue taking turns until the wheelbarrow is empty.
- Put some small toy wheelbarrows, play people, and little blocks in the sand tray.
- Write the numerals from 1 to 10 on index cards. Have a child draw a card, then build a tower with that number of blocks. Or suggest building towers of the numbers in sequential order, or numbers in reverse order.
- Children love wheeling things. Get some big garden pebbles and let them load and wheel them around outside.

On Target

11

Try active learning about shapes by playing toss-it-in-the-box games.

Vocabulary

aim

circle

gently

rectangle

shape

sort

spool

square

throw

toss

triangle

What you need

- 4 large cardboard boxes
- colored paper
- empty smaller boxes, containers, and other materials (see below for suggestions)
- glue or tape
- scissors (adult use only)

Learning objectives

Children will:

- Work as part of a group or class, taking turns and sharing.
- Interact with others, negotiating plans and activities.
- Use language such as "circle" or "bigger" to describe the shape and size of solids and flat shapes.
- Look closely at similarities and differences.
- Develop hand-eye coordination.

Before you start

Cut a large circle, square, rectangle, and triangle from colored paper and glue each shape to one of the cardboard boxes.

Helpful hint

Ask families to bring in lots of empty boxes and containers of various shapes. Put up a notice asking for more unusual items, such as spools (from sewing thread), old buttons, jar lids, bottle tops, and yogurt containers. It may be a challenge to find triangles!

What you do

1. Put the big boxes and all the smaller boxes, containers, and materials on the floor (or outside on the grass or path).

2. Talk to the children about the big boxes, and the shape on each one.

3. Look at the small boxes and other items and ask each child to choose one. Name the shape of each object as a child picks it—for example, bottle tops are circles, and boxes are rectangles or squares. Use simple shape names, instead of the three-dimensional shapes.

4. Take turns tossing each small item into the big box with the right shape on it. (For example, toss a yogurt container and a bottle top into the box with the circle.)

More ideas

- Attach shape stickers to plastic cube blocks for sorting and matching games.
- Make patterns using only blocks of one shape, such as triangles.
- Try rolling and sliding blocks of different shapes along the floor (or down a ramp). Make the game more challenging by aiming for matching chalk shapes on the floor.
- Sort blocks in different ways: according to shape, size, color, or number of corners.
- Build towers of blocks to use for bowling pins. Knock them down with soft balls or beanbags.

Parachute Fun

12

Use soft blocks and practice playing collaboratively with a mini-parachute.

Vocabulary

balance

bounce

careful

corner

down

fabric

high

low

parachute

up

What you need

- squares of soft fabric, about 3 feet on each side
- colored die
- lightweight blocks, fabric or foam

Learning objectives

Children will:

- Work as part of a group, taking turns and sharing.
- Interact with others, negotiating plans and activities.
- Develop their hand-eye coordination.
- Use language that expresses direction: up/down; over/under; in/out.

Before you start

Sit with a group of four children, each holding a corner of the fabric. Practice working together to lift the fabric high and bring it down low. Try balancing a teddy bear in the fabric and taking it up and down without dropping it.

Helpful hint

Try using beanbags or rolled-up pairs of socks instead of fabric blocks.

What you do

1. Four children sit on the floor holding the corners of the fabric. Several games can go on at once.
2. Each group rolls the die and names the color that comes up. They then find a block of that color and put it in the middle of the fabric.

③ Holding the corners of the fabric, children work together to see how long they can bounce their block up and down without bouncing it off the fabric!

④ Roll the die again and add a second block. Start the game again. See if children can manage a third block. The aim of the game is to work together to see how long they can go on, and to see how high they can bounce the blocks.

More ideas

- Stretch the cloth taut and build a tower of two or three blocks on it. *Slowly* raise the fabric. How high can the children raise the cloth go before the tower topples over?

- Hold the fabric a few inches above the floor. Ask one child to wriggle under and find blocks of different shapes or colors.

- Throw lots of blocks under a big parachute and let each child, in turn, run under the parachute to collect a named number or color of blocks—for example, "two yellow" or "three red."

- Put lots of soft blocks on a big parachute and work together in a large group to keep them in the air.

Nesting Boxes

Put tiny surprises and hidden treasures inside boxes that nest inside each other, like nesting dolls.

Vocabulary

biggest/bigger

box

hiding/hidden

inside

lid

names of the
objects you are
using

nesting

order

size

smallest/smaller

top

What you need

- set of boxes that fit inside each other
- small everyday objects, such as: a coin, a shell, a button, a paper clip, a spoon, a small car, and a key

button   small car

spoon

paper clip

key

shell   coin

Learning objectives

Children will:

- Maintain attention and concentration when necessary.
- Use a widening vocabulary to express their ideas and observations.
- Investigate objects and materials by using all of their senses.
- Use language that expresses direction: up/down; over/under; in/out.

Before you start

Let the children explore the empty boxes and see how they nest inside each other. Explore finding and fitting the right lid on each box. Practice arranging the boxes in size order.

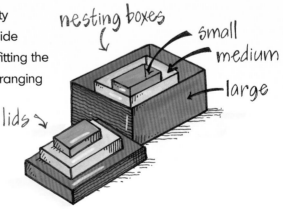

nesting boxes

small
medium
large

lids

Helpful hint

Craft stores and IKEA sell sets of nesting boxes, which are ideal for this activity.

What you do

① Hide an everyday object inside each box.

② Ask each child to choose a box and peek inside.

③ Now take turns: each child describes the object in her box by its use, shape, and color so the other children can guess what it is. Some children may find this hard and need a bit of help with the descriptions.

④ Now put the boxes in order of size. Can the children remember what is in the biggest box? Take turns guessing (or remembering) what is in each box.

⑤ Open each box in turn, and describe the surprise inside.

More ideas

● Play the game with natural objects, such as leaves, flowers, twigs, and seeds.

● Play "The One That Doesn't Belong" by, for example, putting cars in all but one box and a toy animal as the one that doesn't belong.

● Provide different types of treasures, such as ribbons, shells, sequins, buttons, and jewelry, to use in the boxes.

● Hide different name cards or pictures in the boxes.

● Hide the boxes around the room or outside. Have a Treasure Box Hunt to find them all. Check by nesting the boxes together again to see if any are missing.

● Build a tower of the boxes, starting with the largest on the bottom and piling them up in order of size.

14 Treasure Hunt

Hide blocks in the sand and hunt for letters and names.

Vocabulary

alphabet

blocks

bury

find

hide

hunt

initials

letters

name

sand

search

What you need

- alphabet blocks
- index cards
- pen
- sand and sand tray

Learning objectives

Children will:

- Hear and say sounds and recognize first letters of their names.
- Develop their hand-eye coordination.

Before you start

Write each child's name on an index card.

Helpful hint

If you have plastic blocks that you are willing to write on with a permanent marker, you can play this game in the water as well.

What you do

1. Talk to the children about the game, explaining how it works and what to do.
2. Bury all the blocks in the sand.
3. Then, help the children find their own name cards and look at the first letters in their names.
4. Have the children hunt in the sand, looking for blocks with their letters.

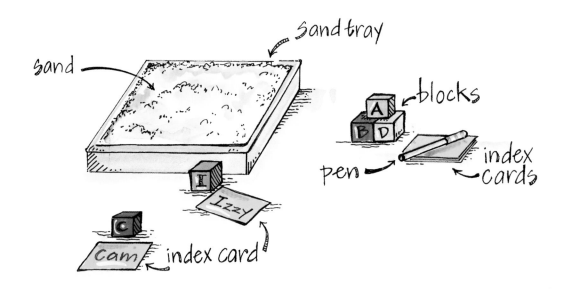

⑤ Try it with someone else's name card. This is much more difficult!

⑥ Bury the blocks again. Have each child pick one. Can you think of someone's name that starts with the letter on the block you picked?

⑦ Play the game again with the initial letters of classroom toys: car, truck, doll, and so on.

More ideas

- Roll and cut out letters from your favorite recipe for playdough. Bake these, paint and varnish them, and bury them in the sand.
- Hide blocks with letters or pictures (or both) outside for the children to find.
- Older children may like to hunt in the sand for all the letters of their names.
- Make blocks into towers and trains that spell out names.
- Fish in the water tray for names written on small blocks. Use nets from a pet store for the fishing.

Collector's Case

Use large, flat boxes and create portfolio-like cases to keep precious artwork safe.

Vocabulary

artist
box
carry
case
decorate
keep
portfolio
safe
save

What you need

- assorted craft materials, such as feathers, sequins, scraps of paper and fabric
- crayons
- flat cardboard boxes with lids, 1 per child (unused pizza boxes work particularly well)
- glue
- large paintbrushes
- markers
- newspaper to cover the work surface
- paint
- smocks

Learning objectives

Children will:

- Explore color, texture, and form.
- Use a range of materials with increasing control.
- Use simple tools and techniques competently and appropriately.
- Maintain attention and concentration when necessary.
- Express and communicate ideas about designing and making.

Before you start

Collect the boxes you will need. Ask at a local pizza shop. They might be very happy to donate clean, unused boxes for this project.

child's name ← pizza box

child's artwork

decorated box

What you do

① Write the children's names on their boxes in bold print, using colorful markers. (Do this on the inside of the lid.)

② Cover the floor or a large surface with newspaper and ask the children to wear smocks.

③ Have the children color or paint the outside of their boxes.

④ When the boxes are dry, invite the children to decorate them with an assortment of materials.

⑤ Use the boxes to store the children's artwork and to transport fragile materials home over the course of the year.

More ideas

● Talk about artists and artists' portfolios. Is there a museum or a studio nearby that you could visit as a class?

● Cut or tear strips of fabric to use as ties for the portfolios. Tearing fabric is very satisfying!

16 In the Clear

Use transparent construction materials for a really different experience.

Vocabulary

attach

build

clear

construct

fasten

see-through

transparent

What you need

- child-safe scissors
- clear plastic bottles
- clear plastic boxes (for example, berry boxes, other boxes from the produce section of the supermarket)
- clear plastic cups
- clear plastic straws
- clear plastic trays
- clear plastic tubing
- clear tape
- colored cellophane
- foil
- food coloring
- glitter
- glue
- plastic bubble wrap

Learning objectives

Children will:

- Be confident enough to try new activities.
- Interact with others, negotiating plans and activities.
- Use language such as "circle" and "bigger" to describe the shapes and comparative sizes of solids and flat shapes.
- Build and construct with a wide range of objects, selecting appropriate resources and adapting their work where necessary.
- Explore color, texture, and form.

Helpful hints

- Try hardware stores, pet stores, stationery stores, and kitchenware stores for transparent materials.
- Ask parents to look around at home and in the community for suitable resources, and put out a transparent container to collect their contributions.

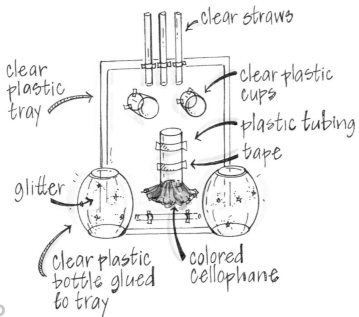

clear straws

clear plastic tray

clear plastic cups

plastic tubing

tape

glitter

clear plastic bottle glued to tray

colored cellophane

What you do

1 Let the children explore the materials in free play. What else can they think of that is transparent? (For example: the fish tank, the windows, jars).

2 Encourage the children to experiment with putting materials together and figuring out ways to attach them to each other. Offer support and encouragement, but let them explore independently.

3 Use the food coloring to make colored water. Help the children add this to the bottles and sealed containers in their constructions. Experiment with glitter and foil in the water.

4 Encourage the children to select their own resources and try out their own ideas. Play alongside them, making comments and asking open-ended questions. Encourage the children to talk about the transparent materials.

More ideas

● Put clear and transparent objects in the water tray, with clear, colored, or bubbly water.

● Have other themed construction sessions: try shiny, reflective materials; rough or smooth textured materials; or long, thin materials like boxes and ribbon, string, straws, raffia, and paper strips.

● Use colored cellophane to make transparent pictures for mobiles and window pictures. You can also make colored glasses!

● Make a huge transparent model by working as a group.

Roll the Dice

17

Jump, crawl, tiptoe, twirl, and hop. Pay attention, so you know when it is your turn.

Vocabulary

crawl
dice
finish
giant
hop
jump
skip
start
tiptoe
twirl

What you need

- block or box with square sides (You may need more than one, depending on the size of your group. You need a side for every starting letter in your children's names.)
- chalk or masking tape
- markers

Learning objectives

Children will:

- Work as part of a group or class, taking turns and sharing.
- Link sounds with letters.
- Move with confidence and imagination.

Helpful hint

If you do not have a cube-shaped block or box, copy the template on page 73. (You may need more than one, depending on the size of your group, see "What you need," above.) Cut them out and glue them to card stock. Fold and glue the sides in place, and leave to dry before using.

What you do

1. Use the chalk or masking tape to mark a start and a finish line about 10 feet apart on the floor.
2. Write the first letter of each child's name on one face of the block or box dice.
3. The children will take turns rolling the dice. Change the action for each turn— for example, bunny hops, skipping, long jumps, twirling, crawling, walking on tiptoe, or giant strides.

30 Fun Ways to Learn with Blocks and Boxes

4. Roll one die. The children whose names begin with the letter that comes up travel from the start to the finish line using the action you have selected. This is not a race. The object is for everyone to complete the course. Everyone can be successful.

5. Continue rolling the dice until each child has had a turn to cross the finish line.

6. Play a return round, if you like.

More ideas

- Make a pile of small blocks. Take turns rolling a number die and toss that number of blocks into a bucket or bowl. Continue until all the blocks are in the bucket.

- Make a color die. Ask all the children to lie on the floor. Roll the die and say the color. All the children wearing that color stand up. Continue until everyone is standing.

- Draw an item of dress-up clothing on each face of a box or die—for example, a hat, shoes, a coat, gloves, boots, and a scarf. The children take turns rolling the die and putting on the item of clothing. Continue until the dress-up box is empty!

Mail Those Letters!

18

Practice writing and recognizing numerals as you prepare and deliver the mail.

Vocabulary

address
block/blocks
box/boxes
build
envelope
house
house number
letter
letter carrier
mail box
mail slot
stamp

What you need

- blocks
- cereal boxes
- envelopes
- markers, pens, and crayons
- postcards, or index cards to use as postcards
- sharp scissors or craft knife (adult use only)
- sticky notes

Learning objectives

Children will:

- Interact with others, negotiating plans and activities.
- Say and understand number names.
- Recognize the numerals 1 to 9.
- Observe the places where they live.
- Develop their hand-eye coordination.

Before you start

Go for a walk and look at front doors, mailboxes, and house numbers. Notice what the mail boxes look like. How many different shapes do you see? Make a list of some of the numbers you see.

Helpful hint

Carefully open up the cereal boxes, turn them inside out and glue them back together. This gives a clean plain surface for the children to work on.

large
appliance
box

envelope

checking
address

sticky
notes

5 2 1

mail slot

What you do

1. Build several block houses.

2. Cut mail slots in the cereal boxes (adult step only). Now the children can paint and decorate the mailboxes.

3. Use a marker to number the houses with sticky notes. Number the mailboxes and put one by each house you have made.

4. Make a matching set of numbers on the postcards. Cut some of the postcards into smaller cards so they will fit into the mailbox openings. Number these cards, too.

5. Give each child a pile of postcards to deliver to the mailboxes. Match the numbers on the cards with the numbers on the houses.

6. You could make a row of child-sized houses from big appliance boxes. Paint them with acrylic paints, cut (adult-only step) doors and windows, and mail slots in the doors. Add house numbers and deliver mail to these houses.

More ideas

- Cover a large box with blue paper or paint it blue, to make a mailbox. Cut a large slit for mailing envelopes and packages. Put this near the dramatic play center, and provide pens, cards, used envelopes, and play stamps. Add a mail bag and a light blue shirt for the letter carrier.

- Set up the train track. Add a few trucks and vans, play people, and some tiny cards and letters to carry in the trains and trucks.

19 Bridge Builder

Build real bridges across a tray of water for cars, trains, and people.

Vocabulary

bridge

harbor

pillar

railway

road

span

train

tube

tunnel

vehicle

What you need

- blocks and planks
- cars and boats
- long cardboard tubes
- plastic/wooden train set
- sand and stones
- shallow water tray or builder's tray
- small toy people

Learning objectives

Children will:

- Be interested, excited, and motivated to learn.
- Build and construct, selecting resources and adapting work where necessary.

Before you start

Completely cover the cardboard tubes with clear contact paper to make them last longer.

Helpful hint

You need less than an inch of water in the tray. Add some pebbles, shells, and water creatures to make it more fun.

What you do

1. Build a "harbor" in the water tray with blocks, sand, and stones. Do not make the water too deep.

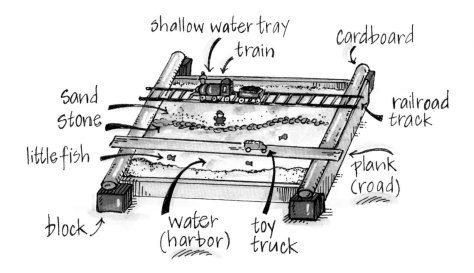

shallow water tray
train

cardboard

sand
stone

railroad
track

little fish

plank
(road)

block

water
(harbor)

toy
truck

2. Arrange the planks across the tray as road bridges.

3. Rest the cardboard tubes on block pillars built on each side, outside of the tray, so the tube spans the tray.

4. Set up the train track and build a train bridge across the tray.

5. Add people, boats, and vehicles to use the roads and bridges you have built.

6. Talk with the children about how you can improve the bridges and roads across the harbor. Try resting the tube bridges on pillars of different heights so you can send trains and cars through the sloping tubes.

More ideas

- Cut holes in the sides of ice cream tubs, turn them over, and cover them with sand to make tunnels in the sand tray. Add short pieces of drainpipe and guttering. Then add diggers and dump trucks for further excavations.

- Use shoeboxes and small cardboard boxes on the floor to create tunnels for your train set.

- Use boxes and blocks to build barns and enclosures for small zoo or farm animals.

- Shoeboxes make great stations, platforms, and farm buildings.

20 Cars, Buses, and Trucks

Create interesting roads, tunnels, and bridges with cardboard materials of all kinds.

Vocabulary

automobile

bridge

bus

car

drive

ramp

road

travel

trip

truck

vehicle

What you need

- card stock
- cardboard tubes
- corrugated cardboard
- large cardboard boxes
- masking tape
- saw or box cutter (adult use only)
- toy vehicles

Learning objectives

Children will:

- Work as part of a group or class, taking turns and sharing.
- Interact with others, negotiating plans and activities.
- Use simple tools and techniques competently and appropriately.
- Develop their hand-eye coordination.

Before you start

Go for a walk and look at some roads and moving vehicles.

Helpful hint

Try copying and shipping stores, fabric stores, or carpet suppliers for tubes and cardboard packaging materials. Ask parents for donations.

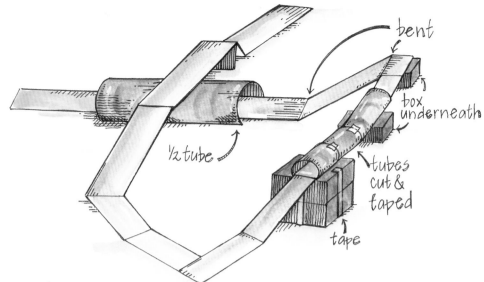

bent

box underneath

½ tube

tubes cut & taped

tape

What you do

1. Cut some of the cardboard tubes in half lengthwise. (Safety note: You will need a saw or a sharp box cutter for carpet tubes. Do this when the children are not present.) Open up some of the boxes and use the cardboard to make steep ramps.

2. Use the halved tubes to create long tunnels.

3. Stack two boxes and attach them together with tape. Glue or tape one end of a whole tube to the top box to create a long ramp.

4. Open the sides of two boxes and tape them together to form a long tunnel.

5. Use markers, chalk, or masking tape to make roads between and inside the tunnels and ramps. If you use really big boxes, the children can crawl through the tunnels with their vehicles.

More ideas

- Stack some boxes and add ramps to make a multi-story parking lot.
- Use tiny boxes and containers as freight.
- Provide small pens and pads to record journeys and deliveries, license plates, and names.
- Make tiny license plates on sticky notes.
- Use more boxes to make a gas station, a police station, a school, houses, and apartment buildings.
- Make road and street signs, stop signs, and traffic lights, using cardboard, craft sticks, and markers.

21 Over, Under, and Through

Have fun creeping, crawling, wriggling, slithering, and sliding through an obstacle course made from boxes.

Vocabulary

crawl

creep

obstacle

over

slide

slither

tent

through

tunnel

under

wriggle

What you need

- chalk
- dress-up clothes
- lightweight blanket or sheet
- large cardboard boxes
- large pieces of fabric
- masking tape

Learning objectives

Children will:

- Dress and undress with increasing independence.
- Explore with all their senses.
- Move in a range of ways.
- Use language that expresses direction: up/down; over/under; in/out.

Before you start

Gather the materials you will need. The children can practice wriggling, sliding, and other movements on the ground while you make the preparations.

Helpful hint

Call local appliance and electronics stores to request large boxes and cartons from items such as TVs and washing machines.

What you do

1. Make sure the floor is dry and clean.

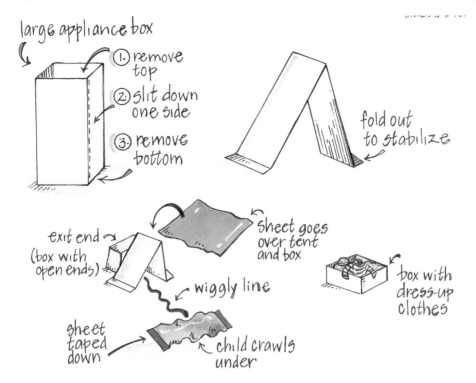

large appliance box

1. remove top
2. slit down one side
3. remove bottom

fold out to stabilize

sheet goes over tent and box

exit end (box with open ends)

wiggly line

box with dress-up clothes

sheet taped down

child crawls under

2 Open out some of the boxes to create tent-like structures.

3 Chalk or tape a wiggly line on the ground or floor.

4 Spread and tape a blanket or sheet to the floor a little way down the line. Make it slack enough for the children to wriggle under.

5 Place the cardboard tent next, and then drape fabric over another box with open ends for the children to crawl through.

6 Have a box of dress-up clothes at the starting point.

7 Help each child put on one item from the box (they choose) and set off down the obstacle course, wriggling and slithering along the ground and trying not to wobble off the line.

More ideas

- When the children get to the end, they can come around again and put on another piece of clothing for another turn.

- Let several children go down the course together so they need to collaborate and negotiate.

- Use a pile of stuffed animals instead of dress-up clothes for the children to take down the course.

- Join several boxes together to make a long, dark tunnel, and provide some flashlights to light the way.

A Basket of Boxes

Explore a basket full of treasure boxes.

Vocabulary

bell

explore

find

hide

jewel

key

polished stone

other words

  naming the

  treasures you

  have chosen

sequin

treasure

trinket

What you need

- shallow basket
- tiny boxes
- trinkets and interesting objects such as coins, keys, jewels, tiny toys, shells, spices, seeds, petals, and sequins to put inside the boxes. Include objects that the children can explore using all their senses: perfumed and scented objects, aromatic herbs, jingle bells, different textures, rough stone, polished marble, and so on.

Learning objectives

Children will:

- Investigate objects and materials by using all of their senses as appropriate.
- Develop their hand-eye coordination.
- Explore color, texture, and form.
- Use a widening vocabulary to express their ideas and observations.

Before you start

Ask the children, parents, colleagues, and friends to help you collect small boxes.

Helpful hint

If you have trouble finding enough tiny boxes, consider using little drawstring bags, decorated folded envelopes, or any other small, appealing containers.

beads
coins
dill seeds
sparkly buttons
keys
tiny bells
mint leaves
cinnamon sticks
small pieces of sandpaper
tiny boxes
treasure basket
marbles
rosemary
pieces of sponge

What you do

1. Set up the treasure basket with all of the tiny boxes and any other containers you are using.

2. Give the children plenty of time to explore the contents of the basket slowly and carefully.

3. Stay close by to share the children's pleasure in the objects. Listen to what they say and encourage them to feel, smell, explore, and enjoy each object.

4. Reflect back to the children their comments about the treasure, modeling descriptive language.

5. Encourage the children to handle the objects carefully and to replace them in the boxes. Then put the boxes back in the treasure basket.

6. Leave the treasure basket out and available so that the children can explore it individually, as well as in small groups.

More ideas

- Invite the children to bring in tiny objects from home to add to the treasure basket.
- Add tiny notes to the treasure basket for the children to discover.
- Invite the children to choose a favorite treasure item and bring it to group or circle time.
- Provide some wrapping paper, small boxes, and tape in the art center or the dramatic play center so the children can make surprise treasure gifts for each other.
- Carefully take apart some boxes and envelopes, and look at how they are made. Try making your own boxes with the children.

Texture Blocks

Explore these boxes with all the senses.

Vocabulary

bumpy

corrugated

fabric

foil

fuzzy

slippery

smooth

soft

rough

What you need

- glue
- materials with interesting textures, for example: sandpaper, foil, corrugated cardboard, bubble wrap, crumpled tissue, fuzzy fabric
- sharp scissors (adult use only)
- small boxes

Learning objectives

Children will:

- Interact with others, negotiating plans and activities.
- Use a widening vocabulary to express their ideas and observations.
- Investigate objects and materials by using all of their senses.
- Explore color, texture, and form.
- Develop their hand-eye coordination.

Before you start

Ask families to send in small, sturdy boxes. The more you have for this project, the more involved the children can become. Cut the various materials into pieces that will fit on the tops and bottoms of the boxes you have collected.

What you do

1 Get out the materials and cover your work surface with newspaper or an old plastic tablecloth.

2 Invite the children to help you glue the textured materials onto the boxes. The top and bottom of the same box should have the same material.

glued
together

furry
material

sandpaper

3 You may want several choices of glue. Glue sticks will work well for some materials, but small containers of white glue and small brushes may be better for others.

4 Glue the lids closed.

5 Once the glue is dry, you have a set of interesting, textured, box-blocks to build with in the block area.

More ideas

- You and the children could glue textured material inside small boxes with lids for a different texture exploration experience. If you do this, do not glue the lids closed!

- Give each of the children a shoebox and invite them to create individualized texture collages inside their boxes. These collages could include color and small objects as well.

24 Up the Steps

Build steps and stairs to practice problem solving.

Vocabulary

count
height
high
many
number
staircase
stairs
steep
stepstool
tower

What you need

- Legos® or similar modular blocks (any size)
- play people
- ribbon or yarn
- scissors (adult use only)
- wooden blocks

Learning objectives

Children will:

- Interact with others, negotiating plans and activities.
- Say and understand number names.
- Build and construct with a wide range of objects.
- Develop their hand-eye coordination.

Before you start

If your center has steps or stairs, number them with labels that can be attached securely at child height. Get in the habit of chanting, whispering, singing, and saying the numbers as you go up and down the stairs.

Helpful hint

Visit thrift shops or watch the classified ads and bargain websites for sets of second-hand plastic blocks. Disinfect with a dilute bleach solution, then wash and rinse well before using.

ribbon

walking the people up the stairs

What you do

1. Show the children how to make steps with different kinds of blocks and give them time to practice in free play.

2. Cut a short piece of yarn or ribbon and help the children make a staircase the same height as the ribbon. There will be many "right" ways to do this.

3. Walk the play people up the steps, counting as you go.

4. Now make another staircase the same height, using a different kind of blocks. How many steps does it have?

5. Cut more lengths of ribbon and do it again. Can you guess how many steps without counting?

6. Build a small tower with big blocks. Make some staircases to climb up the tower. Make a bigger tower and try again.

More ideas

- Make a striped staircase with steps of alternating colors.
- Put numbers on sticky labels and number the steps in your staircases.
- Make an alphabet staircase with a letter on each step.
- Put one play person on the first step, two on the second step, three on the third step, and so on.
- Make stairs for a dollhouse, steps for the animals to get into Noah's Ark, or a stairway to a toy airplane.
- Ask parents to help you make some big steps outside with railroad ties, concrete blocks, or paving stones. You do not need a slope—children will love steps that just go up and then come down again.

25 Through the Maze

Use blocks and boxes to create a maze.

Vocabulary

challenging

confusing

labyrinth

maze

path

roadway

trail

tunnel

turn

twist

What you need

- farm or zoo animals
- masking tape
- play people
- small blocks
- small boxes
- toy trucks and vehicles

Learning objectives

Children will:

- Talk about what they see and experience.
- Move with control and coordination.
- Move with confidence.

Before you start

Sit with the children and share the book *Trail: Paper Poetry Pop-Up* by David Pelham. This magical pop-up book will introduce the children to mazes. Collect some interesting boxes.

Helpful hint

Make your mazes more creative by using interesting play surfaces. Try covering the table or floor with fabric, shiny paper, bubble wrap, corrugated cardboard, or textured paper.

start

What you do

1. Open some of the boxes to make tunnels.

2. Use the blocks and small boxes to make a maze of roadways for the cars and trucks to drive through. You can glue them down or leave them to be rearranged by the children.

3. Set up the animals on one side of the maze. The children can drive a truck through the maze to collect animals and bring them back.

4. Add tunnels and dead ends to make the maze more challenging. Use your judgement about this. The level of challenge must be appropriate to the ages of your children.

5. The children will enjoy building their own mazes with the boxes and blocks. They could design them on paper first, or draw a map of the mazes afterwards, if you want an extra challenge.

More ideas

- Chalk a maze on the ground outdoors for the children to walk or run through, or to ride through on bikes, cars, and scooters. Add traffic cones and boxes to negotiate.

- Use wooden blocks and a small rake to draw mazes through dry sand for small cars.

- Use appliance boxes to create a maze for the children to crawl and slither through. Add dress-up clothes or curtains to make things more challenging. Give the children sticky notes and pens so they can leave little messages, arrows, and directions in the maze to help others.

26 Box Cars

Build cars, buses, trains, and trucks for imaginative play.

Vocabulary

carriage

control panel

dial

license plate

steering wheel

switch

trailer

train

truck

vehicle

What you need

- bottle tops
- brad-type fasteners
- cardboard
- foil
- glue, paper, pens, and child-safe scissors
- large cardboard boxes
- paint
- paper plates

Learning objectives

Children will:

- Interact with others, negotiating plans and activities.
- Use simple tools and techniques competently and appropriately.
- Build and construct with a range of objects, selecting appropriate materials and adapting work where necessary.
- Design and make things.

Before you start

Be sure you have boxes large enough for at least one child to sit inside. Check that there are no staples or other fastenings to get caught on.

Helpful hint

Use two boxes of a similar size nested inside each other for extra strength.

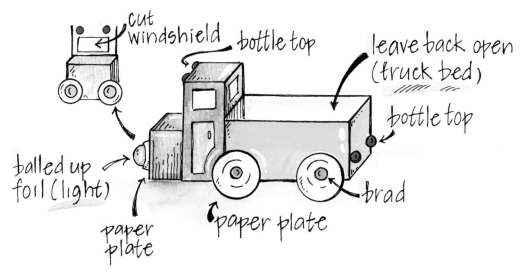

cut windshield

bottle top

leave back open (truck bed)

bottle top

balled up foil (light)

brad

paper plate

paper plate

What you do

1. Talk with the children about the vehicles they want to make.

2. Together, paint the outside of the vehicle, then add paper-plate wheels and foil headlights.

3. Add a control panel with bottle-top dials and switches.

4. Add a paper plate or cardboard steering wheel, attaching it with a brad-type fastener so it will turn.

5. Make license plates for the front and back of the vehicle, and add rear lights and blinkers.

6. Make some traffic lights and road signs, and off you go!

More ideas

- Cut out the bottom of the box and add ribbon shoulder straps so the children can wear the vehicle instead of sitting in it.

- Make a bus stop where passengers can climb aboard (or hold on) behind the vehicle.

- Make a train—you could have several carriages running along behind or set out in a row. Make some train tickets.

- Use two boxes to make a truck so the children can load and carry things.

- Mark out tracks, roads, and railway lines on the floor or outdoors so the children can follow, stop, and start.

- Add some dress-up clothes, including hats and badges for police and traffic officers.

At the Zoo

Add a new spin to zoo play with blocks and boxes.

Vocabulary

animals

bedding

cage

enclosure

endangered

feed

fence

habitat

shelter

zoo

What you need

- blocks
- blue cellophane
- bubble wrap
- burlap
- corrugated cardboard
- raffia and wood shavings
- scissors, tape, and glue
- small boxes (all kinds and sizes)
- zoo animals

Learning objectives

Children will:

- Work as part of a group or class, taking turns and sharing.
- Use a range of materials with increasing control.
- Design and make things.
- Develop their hand-eye coordination.
- Express and communicate ideas about designing and making.

Before you start

Ask parents to collect these materials at home and at work.

Helpful hint

Visit craft stores and fabric stores for fabric remnants.

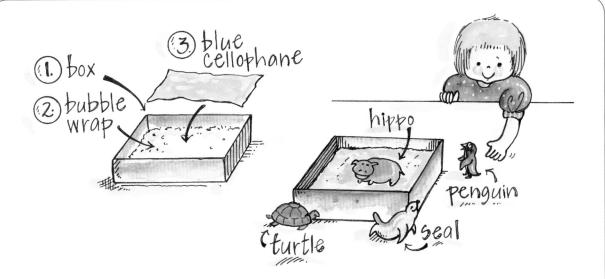

What you do

1. Cover the table top with cardboard.
2. Working with the children, set out the animals and build cages and shelters from boxes and blocks.
3. Make fences and enclosures with strips of cardboard.
4. Use raffia and wood shavings for bedding, and burlap to make doors, sticking it to the boxes with tape or glue.
5. Fill a box with pieces of bubble wrap and cover it with blue cellophane to make a pool for seals and penguins.
6. Play alongside the children, offering commentary and asking open-ended questions.
7. Add some play people as visitors and zoo keepers.

More ideas

- Make signs for the different shelters and enclosures.
- Cut pictures of animals from magazines and catalogs to glue to the shelters.
- Use toy animals and zoo books to make a zoo shop.
- Create a map of the zoo, drawing a picture of each animal in its enclosure.
- Use boxes to make a cafe, a visitor center, the zoo entrance, and the ticket office.
- Make a parking lot for cars and buses.
- Deliver food for the animals in trucks and wheelbarrows.
- If you can arrange it, try to visit a real zoo with the children.

28 Alphabet Treasure

Alphabet collection boxes linked to the first letter of a child's name reinforce the link between letters and the sounds they make.

Vocabulary

alphabet

card

collect

collection

initial

letter

match/matching

name

object

sort/sorting

What you need

- colored paper
- everyday objects and toys
- paint
- plastic, wood, or cardboard letters
- scissors (adult use only)
- shoeboxes, 1 per child

Learning objectives

Children will:

- Work as part of a group or class, taking turns and sharing.
- Link sounds and letters.
- Develop their hand-eye coordination.

Before you start

Cut the first letter of each child's name out of colored paper and set these large letters aside for now. Be sure you have a name card for each child.

Helpful hint

Ask families to send in shoeboxes.

What you do

1. Collect enough shoeboxes for the number of children in the group.
2. Let the children help you cover each shoebox with colored paper, then use the plastic, wood, or cardboard letters and paint to print all over them.

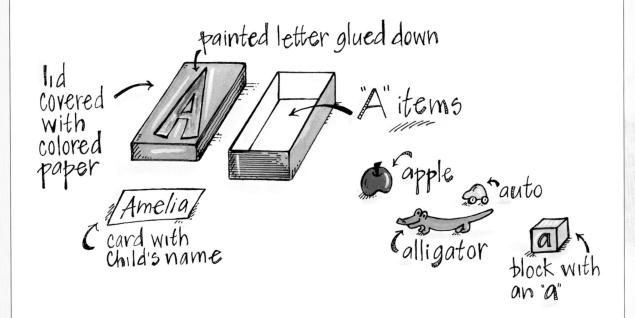

lid covered with colored paper

painted letter glued down

"A" items

apple

auto

alligator

block with an "a"

Amelia

card with child's name

③ Now, glue each child's large letter on the lid of her box.

④ Help the children collect objects and toys that begin with the initial letters of their own names.

⑤ When all the boxes are filled, dump everything out and, working together, sort the objects back into their correct boxes, saying the child's name each time a toy is placed in her box.

More ideas

● Play the game again, this time asking each child to find an object that is a particular color and begins with the first letter of her name.

● Get out the name cards for the whole group and let each child find her own name, then put it in her box with the other objects.

● Ask for adult volunteers to make a set of drawstring bags, each one about four inches on a side. Sew or glue a felt or fabric letter to each bag. Use these for collecting letters or objects, or for sorting the name cards by their initial letters.

● Use an alphabet floor mat as a focus for collecting objects for each letter sound.

Straws and More

Build lightweight other-worldly structures with unusual materials and fasteners.

Vocabulary

clip
connect
construct
fasten
needle
ribbon
string
thread
yarn

What you need

- binder clips
- buttons
- card stock
- children's blunt threading needles
- paper clips
- pipe cleaners
- ribbon, thread, and string
- single-hole punch
- small cardboard boxes
- straws

Learning objectives

Children will:

- Maintain attention and concentration when necessary.
- Use simple tools and techniques competently and appropriately.
- Build and construct with a wide range of objects, selecting appropriate materials and adapting work where necessary.
- Express and communicate ideas in designing and making.

Before you start

Make sure the children know how to use the hole punch, threading needles, and clips safely. **Safety note:** Supervise carefully if you have children who might put things into their mouths.

Helpful hint

Keep your box of interesting scraps handy so the children can add other things to their creations.

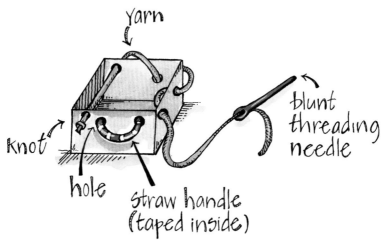

yarn

knot

hole

straw handle
(taped inside)

blunt
threading
needle

What you do

1. Give the children plenty of time freely to explore the materials before they start building.

2. Get the children thinking by punching holes in the small cardboard boxes and pieces of cardstock so they can be threaded together with string, yarn, or pipe cleaners.

3. Sit with the children and play alongside them, exploring the materials yourself and talking about them. Ask open-ended questions, but try not to influence the construction.

4. Encourage the children to share ideas and techniques for joining the materials.

5. Help the children choose additional materials and resources for their constructions.

6. Be available to help with holding, cutting, and steadying the models as they emerge.

More ideas

- Give the children a challenge. Ask, for example, "Can we build a chain? A tower? A wizard's castle?"
- Add small amounts of modeling material such as clay or playdough.
- Offer crayons, markers, paint, and glue for decorating.
- Introduce play people, vehicles, and animals to add new possibilities to the constructions.
- Suggest that the children could link their small structures into a huge one by joining them with straws, pipe cleaners, paper strips, or tape; or try making a really big collaborative structure from these light materials.

30 Creative Community

Build your own miniature community in a shoebox.

Vocabulary

build/building
city
community
construct
create
house
library
school
store
town
trees
village

What you need

- child-safe scissors
- construction paper
- glue
- markers
- shoeboxes, 1 per child
- small boxes to use inside the shoeboxes

Learning objectives

Children will:

- Interact with others, and negotiate plans and activities.
- Express and communicate ideas in designing and making.
- Develop their hand-eye coordination.

Before you start

Invite parents, caretakers, and other family members to collect and send in shoeboxes. You will need one per child. You will also need a good assortment of tiny boxes to use as houses and buildings.

What you do

1. Give each child a shoebox.
2. Have the children plan what buildings and details they would like to include in the community that they will create in the shoebox. (Note: You can use the shoebox on its side, like a small stage, or you can work inside the box to make an enclosed setting.)

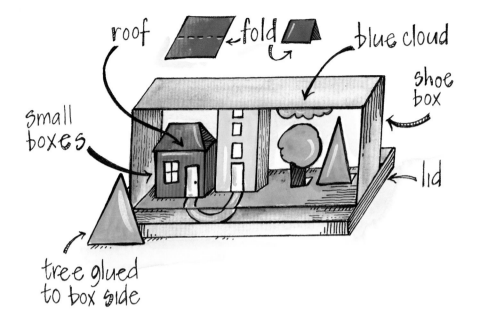

roof ←fold blue cloud

shoe box

small boxes

lid

tree glued to box side

3️⃣ Provide the children with construction paper, very small boxes, scissors, markers, and glue so that they can create buildings, trees, and landmarks and decorate them.

4️⃣ Show the children how to fold the bottoms of their cutouts to form a tab for the glue.

5️⃣ Have the children glue everything into their boxes. Stay nearby and offer help as needed.

More ideas

● Go on a walking tour of your community. Visit places such as the local bakery, police station, fire station, and doctor's office.

● Have the class work together to make a map of the community or neighborhood. Let the children draw streets, buildings, and parks. Encourage them to add their homes to the map.

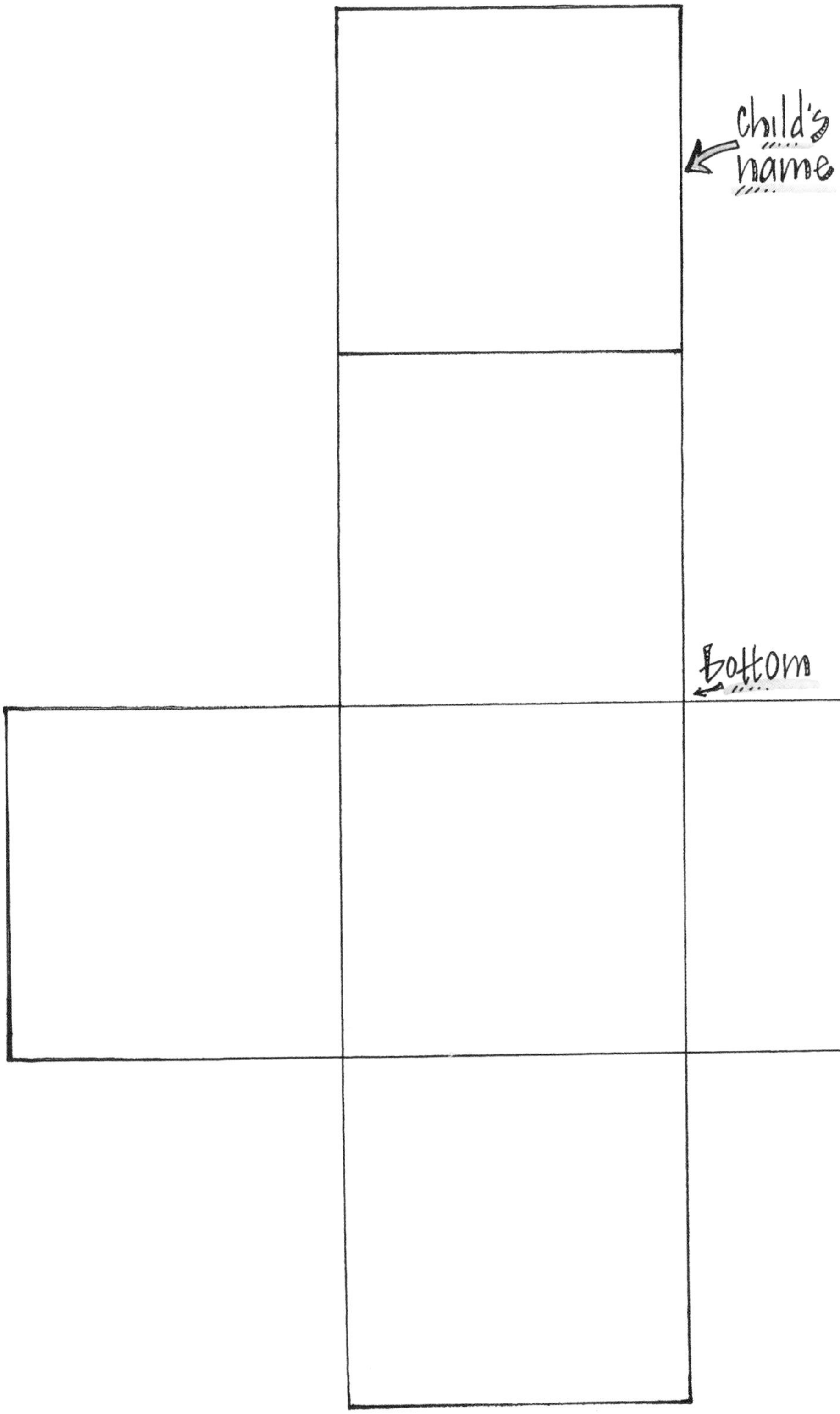

← Child's
name

← Bottom

box template

Index